Masonic & Rosicrucian
History

By Manly P. Hall &
Harold Voorhis

ISBN: 978-1-63118-486-4

Foundations of Freemasonry
Series

Other Books in this Series and Related Titles

Table of Contents

INTRODUCTION

From the beginning of Modern Freemasonry's birthdate of 1717, the intelligentsia of humanity have found refuge for safe reflection within the walls of the fraternity. Masonic writers have produced a nearly incalculable amount of written musings on a multitude of esoteric and philosophical subjects, as they relate to the ancient mysteries that Freemasonry currently storehouses. Sadly, most of it appears to have sat largely unread, as American Freemasonry in particular, continues to transform itself into something that bears little resemblance to what it was originally designed to be. The true essence of Freemasonry is not that of blind patriotism or a single-minded national religion but one of Universal Brotherhood and altruism, designed for the betterment not just of its members but of society as a whole. In particular, for those who are not members of the fraternity, as Freemasonry has always acted as a beacon, to help guide humanity through darker times, with the hopes that one day we will collectively reach a truly enlightened age.

It's not uncommon for new members joining the fraternity to find little education within the walls of many modern lodges, in spite of so much written material available to the membership. Many older members are not simply uneducated with regards to real Masonic history and symbology, not to mention the vast arena of related subjects, but they are disinterested in all of it, as well.

Lamp of Trismegistus is doing its part to help preserve humanity's Masonic history by making some of these classics available to those students who are seeking to unearth the knowledge of these ancient colossi. As such, Lamp of Trismegistus offers its readers highlights of Masonic study, culled from a variety

7

of authors and viewpoints, with the hope bringing education back into the fraternity. So, be sure to check out other titles in our *Foundations of Freemasonry Series* as well as our *Theosophical Classics, Occult Fiction, Paranormal Research Series, Esoteric Classics, Supernatural Fiction, Studies in Buddhism* and our *Christian Apocrypha Series* as well as numerous other subjects; and, don't be afraid to let a little altruism into your own heart or even into your Lodge. You can also download the audio versions of many of these titles from Audible, Amazon or Apple, for learning on the go.

ROSICRUCIAN AND MASONIC ORIGINS

By Manly P. Hall

Freemasonry is a fraternity within a fraternity—an outer organization concealing an inner brotherhood of the elect. Before it is possible to intelligently discuss the origin of the Craft, it is necessary, therefore, to establish the existence of these two separate yet interdependent orders, the one visible and the other invisible. The visible society is a splendid *camaraderie* of "free and accepted" men enjoined to devote themselves to ethical, educational, fraternal, patriotic, and humanitarian concerns. The invisible society is a secret and most august fraternity whose members are dedicated to the service of a mysterious *arcanum arcanorum*. Those Brethren who have essayed to write the history of their Craft have not included in their disquisitions the story of that truly secret inner society which is to the body Freemasonic what the heart is to the body human. In each generation only a few are accepted into the inner sanctuary of the Work, but these are veritable Princes of the Truth and their sainted names shall be remembered in future ages together with the seers and prophets of the elder world. Though the great initiate-philosophers of Freemasonry can be counted upon one's fingers, yet their power is not to be measured by the achievements of ordinary men. They are dwellers upon the Threshold of the Innermost, Masters of that secret doctrine which forms the invisible foundation of every great theological and rational institution.

The outer history of the Masonic order is one of noble endeavor, altruism, and splendid enterprise; the inner history, one of silent conquest, persecution, and heroic martyrdom. The body of Masonry rose from the guilds of workmen who wandered the face of medieval Europe, but the spirit of Masonry walked with God before the universe was spread out or the scroll of the heavens unrolled. The enthusiasm of the young Mason is the effervescence of a pardonable pride. Let him extol the merits of his Craft, reciting its steady growth, its fraternal spirit, and its worthy undertakings. Let him boast of splendid buildings and an ever-increasing sphere of influence. These are the tangible evidence of power and should rightly set a-flutter the heart of the Apprentice who does not fully comprehend as yet that great strength which abides *in* silence or that unutterable dignity to be sensed only by those who have been "raised" into the contemplation of the Inner Mystery.

An obstacle well-nigh insurmountable is to convince the Mason himself that the secrets of his Craft are worthy of his profound consideration. As St. Paul, so we are told, kicked against the "pricks" of conversion, so the rank and file of present-day Masons strenuously oppose any effort put forth to interpret Masonic symbols in the light of philosophy. They are seemingly obsessed by the fear that from their ritualism may be extracted a meaning more profound than is actually contained therein. For years it has been a mooted question whether Freemasonry is actually a religious organization. "Masonry," writes Pike, however, in the *Legenda for the Nineteenth Degree,* "has and always had a religious creed. It teaches what it deems to be the truth in respect to the nature and attributes of God." The more studiously-minded Mason regards the Craft as an aggregation of thinkers concerned with the deeper mysteries of life. The all-too-prominent younger members of the Fraternity, however, if not openly skeptical, are at least indifferent to these weightier issues. The champions of philosophic Masonry, alas, are a weak, small voice which grows weaker and smaller as time goes by. In fact, there are actual *blocs* among the Brethren who would divorce Masonry from both philosophy and religion at any and all cost. If, however, we search the writings of eminent Masons, we find a unanimity of viewpoint: namely, that Masonry is a religious and philosophic body. Every effort initiated to elevate Masonic thought to its true position has thus invariably emphasized the metaphysical and ethical aspects of the Craft.

But a superficial perusal of available documents will demonstrate that the modern Masonic order is not united respecting the true purpose for its own existence. Nor will this factor of doubt be dispelled until the origin of the Craft is established beyond all quibbling. The elements of Masonic history are strangely elusive; there are gaps which apparently cannot be bridged. "Who the early Freemasons really were," states *Gould* in *A Concise History of Freemasonry,* "and whence they came, may afford a tempting theme for inquiry to the speculative antiquary. But it is enveloped in obscurity, and lies far outside the domain of authentic history." Between modern Freemasonry with its vast body of ancient symbolism and those original Mysteries which first employed these symbols there is a dark interval of centuries. To the conservative Masonic historian, the deductions of such writers as Higgins, Churchward, Vail, and Waite—though ingenious and fascinating-actually prove nothing. That Masonry is a body of ancient lore is self-evident, but the tangible "link" necessary to convince the recalcitrant Brethren that their order is the direct successor of the pagan Mysteries has unfortunately not been adduced to date. Of such problems as these is composed the "angel" with which the Masonic Jacob must wrestle throughout the night.

It is possible to trace Masonry back a few centuries with comparative ease, but then the thread suddenly vanishes from sight in a maze of secret societies and political enterprises. Dimly silhouetted in the mists that becloud these tangled issues are such figures as Cagliostro, Comte de St.-Germain, and St. Martin, but even the connection between these individuals and the Craft has never been clearly defined. The writings of early Masonic history is involved in such obvious hazard as to provoke the widespread conclusion that further search is futile. The average Masonic student is content, therefore, to trace his Craft back to the workmen's guilds who chipped and chiseled the cathedrals and public buildings of medieval Europe. While such men as Albert Pike have realized this attitude to be ridiculous, it is one thing to declare it insufficient and quite another to prove the fallacy to an adamantine mind. So much has been lost and forgotten, so much ruled in and out by those unfitted for such legislative revision that the modern rituals do not in every case represent the original rites of the Craft. In his

Symbolism, Pike (*who spent a lifetime in the quest for Masonic secrets*) declares that few of the original meanings of the symbols are known to the modern order, nearly all the so-called interpretations now given being superficial. Pike confessed that the original meanings of the very symbols he himself was attempting to interpret were irretrievably—lost; that even such familiar emblems as the apron and the pillars were locked mysteries, whose "keys" had been thrown away by the uninformed. "The initiated," also writes John Fellows, "as well as those without the pale of the order, are equally ignorant of their derivation and import." (See *Exposition of the Mysteries*)

Preston, Gould, Mackey, Oliver, and Pike—in fact, nearly every great historian of Freemasonry-have all admitted the possibility of the modern society being connected, indirectly at least, with the ancient Mysteries, and their descriptions of the modern society are prefaced by excerpts from ancient writings descriptive of primitive ceremonials. These eminent Masonic scholars have all recognized in the legend of Hiram Abiff an adaptation of the Osiris myth; nor do they deny that the major part of the symbolism of the craft is derived from the pagan institutions of antiquity when the gods were venerated in secret places with strange figures and appropriate rituals. Though cognizant of the exalted origin of their order, these historians-either through fear or uncertainty-have failed, however, to drive home the one point necessary to establish the true purpose of Freemasonry: *They did not realize that the Mysteries whose rituals Freemasonry perpetuates were the custodians of a secret philosophy of life of such transcendent nature that it can only be entrusted to an individual tested and proved beyond all peradventure of human frailty.* The secret schools of Greece and Egypt were neither fraternal nor political fundamentally, nor were their ideals similar to those of the modern Craft. They were essentially philosophic and religious institutions, and all admitted into them were consecrated to the service of the sovereign good. Modern Freemasons, however, regard their Craft primarily as neither philosophic nor religious, but rather as ethical. Strange as it may seem, the majority openly ridicule the very supernatural powers and agencies for which their symbols stand.

The secret doctrine that flows through Freemasonic symbols (*and to whose perpetuation the invisible Masonic body is consecrated*) has its source in three ancient and exalted orders. The first is the Dionysiac artificers, the second the Roman *collegia,* and the third the Arabian Rosicrucians. The Dionysians were the master builders of the ancient world. Originally founded to design and erect the theaters of Dionysus wherein were enacted the tragic dramas of the rituals, this order was repeatedly elevated by popular acclaim to greater dignity until at last it was entrusted with the planning and construction of all public edifices concerned with the commonwealth or the worship of the gods and heroes. Hiram, King of Tyre, was the patron of the Dionysians, who flourished in Tyre and Sidon, and Hiram Abiff (*if we may believe the sacred account*) was himself a Grand Master of this most noble order of pagan builders. King Solomon in his wisdom accepted the services of this famous craftsman, and thus at the instigation of Hiram, King of Tyre, Hiram Abiff, though himself a member of a different faith, journeyed from his own country to design and supervise the erection of the Everlasting House to the true God on Mount

Moriah. The tools of the builders' craft were first employed by the Dionysians as symbols under which to conceal the mysteries of the soul and the secrets of human regeneration. The Dionysians also first likened man to a rough *ashlar* which, trued into a finished block through the instrument of reason, could be fitted into the structure of that living and eternal Temple built without the sound of hammer, the voice of workmen or any tool of contention.

The Roman *collegia* was a branch of the Dionysiacs and to it belonged those initiated artisans who fashioned the impressive monuments whose ruins still lend their immortal glory to the Eternal City. In his *Ten Books on Architecture,* Vitruvius, the initiate of the *collegia,* has revealed that which was permissible concerning the secrets of his holy order. Of the inner mysteries, however, he could not write, for these were reserved for such as had donned the leather apron of the craft. In his consideration of the books now available concerning the Mysteries, the thoughtful reader should note the following words appearing in a twelfth-century volume entitled *Artephil Liber Secretus:* "Is not this an art full of secrets? And believest thou, O fool! that we plainly teach this Secret of Secrets, taking our words according to their literal interpretation?" (See *Sephar H' Debarim.*) Into the stones they trued, the adepts of the *collegia* deeply carved their Gnostic symbols. From earliest times, the initiated stonecutters marked their perfected works with the secret emblems of their crafts and degrees that unborn generations might realize that the master builders of the first ages also labored for the same ends sought by men today.

The Mysteries of Egypt and Persia that had found a haven in the Arabian desert reached Europe by way of the Knights Templars and the Rosicrucians. The Temple of the Rose Cross at Damascus had preserved the secret philosophy of Sharon's Rose; the Druses of the Lebanon still retain the mysticism of ancient Syria; and the dervishes, as they lean on their carved and crotched sticks, still meditate upon the secret instruction perpetuated from the days of the four Caliphs. From the far places of Irak and the hidden retreats of the Sufi mystics, the Ancient Wisdom thus found its way into Europe. Was Jacques de Molay burned by the Holy Inquisition merely because he wore the red cross of the Templar? What were those secrets to which he was true even in death? Did his companion Knights perish with him merely because they had amassed a fortune and exercised an unusual degree of temporal power? To the thoughtless, these may constitute ample grounds, but to those who can pierce the film of the specious and the superficial, they are assuredly insufficient. It was not the physical power of the Templars but the knowledge which they had brought with them from the East that the church feared. The Templars had discovered part of the Great Arcanum; they had become wise in those mysteries which had been celebrated in Mecca thousands of years before the advent of Mohammed; they had read a few pages from the dread book of the *Anthropos,* and for this knowledge they were doomed to die. What was the black magic of which the Templars were accused? What was Baphomet, the Goat of Mendes, whose mysteries they were declared to have celebrated? All these are questions worthy of the thoughtful consideration of every studious Mason.

Truth is eternal. The so-called revelations of Truth that come in different religions are actually but a re-emphasis of an ever-existing doctrine. Thus Moses did not originate a new religion for Israel; he simply adapted the Mysteries of Egypt to the needs of Israel. The ark triumphantly borne by the twelve tribes through the wilderness was copied after the Isaac ark which may still be traced in faint has-relief upon the ruins of the Temple of Philae. Even the two brooding cherubim over the mercy seat are visible in the Egyptian carving, furnishing indubitable evidence that the secret doctrine of Egypt was the prototype of Israel's mystery religion. In his reformation of Indian philosophy, Buddha likewise did not reject the esotericism of the Brahmins, but rather adapted this esotericism to the needs of the masses in India. The mystic secrets locked within the holy Vedas were thus disclosed in order that all men, irrespective of castely distinction, might partake of wisdom and share in a common heritage of good. Jesus was a Rabbin of the Jews, a teacher of the Holy Law, who discoursed in the synagogue, interpreting the Torah according to the teachings of His sect. He brought no new message nor were His reformations radical. He merely tore away the veil from the temple in order that not only Pharisee and Sadducee but also publican and sinner might together behold the glory of an ageless faith.

In his cavern on Mount Hira, Mohammed prayed not for new truths but for old truths to be restated in their original purity and simplicity in order that men might understand again that primitive religion: God's clear revelation to the first patriarchs. The Mysteries of Islam had been celebrated in the great black cube of the Caaba centuries before the holy pilgrimage. The Prophet was but the reformer of a decadent pagandom, the smasher of idols, the purifier of defiled Mysteries. The dervishes, who patterned their garments after those of the Prophet, still preserve that inner teaching of the elect, and for them the *Axis of the Earth* —the supreme hierophant-still sits, visible only to the faithful, in meditation upon the flat roof of the Caaba. Neither carpenter nor cameldriver, as Abdul Baha might have said, can fashion a world religion from the substances of his own mind. Neither prophet nor savior preached a doctrine which was his own, but in language suitable to his time and race retold that Ancient Wisdom preserved within the Mysteries since the dawning of human consciousness. So with the Masonic Mysteries of today. Each Mason has at hand those lofty principles of universal order upon whose certainties the faiths of mankind have ever been established. Each Mason has at hand those lofty principles of universal order upon pregnant with life and hope to those millions who wander in the darkness of unenlightenment. Father C. R. C., the Master of the Rose Cross, was initiated into the Great Work at Damcar. Later at Fez, further information was given him relating to the sorcery of the Arabians. From these wizards of the desert C. R. C. also secured the sacred book M, which is declared to have contained the accumulated knowledge of the world. This volume was translated into Latin by C. R. C. for the edification of his order, but only the initiates know the present hidden repository of the Rosicrucian manuscripts, charters, and manifestos. From the Arabians C. R. C. also learned of the elemental peoples and how, with their aid, it was possible to gain admission to the ethereal world where dwelt the genii and Nature spirits. C. R. C. thus discovered that the magical creatures of the *Arabian Nights Entertainment* actually existed, though invisible to the ordinary mortal. From astrologers living in the desert far from the concourse of the market-place he was further instructed concerning the mysteries of the stars, the virtues resident in the astral light, the rituals of magic and invocation, the preparation of therapeutic talismans, and the binding of the genii. C. R. C. became an adept in the gathering of medicinal herbs, the transmutation of metals, and the manufacture of precious gems by artificial means. Even the secret of the Elixir of Life and the Universal Panacea were communicated to him. Enriched thus beyond the dreams of Croesus, the Holy Master returned to Europe and there established a House of Wisdom which he called *Domus Sancti Spiritus.* This house he enveloped in clouds, it is said, so that men could not discover it. What are these "clouds," however, but the rituals and symbols under which is concealed the Great Arcanum-that unspeakable mystery which every true Mason must seek if he would become in reality a "Prince of the Royal Secret"? Paracelsus, the Swiss Hermes, was initiated into the secrets of alchemy in Constantinople and there beheld the consummation of the *magnum opus.* He is consequently entitled to be mentioned among those initiated by the Arabians into the Rosicrucian work. Cagliostro was also initiated by the Arabians and, because of the knowledge he had thus secured, incurred the displeasure of the Holy See. From the unprobed depths of Arabian Rosicrucianism also issued the illustrious Comte de St.-Germain, over whose Masonic activities to this day hangs the veil of impenetrable mystery. The exalted body of initiates whom he represented, as well as the mission he came to accomplish, have both been concealed from the members of the Craft at large and are apparent only to those few discerning Masons who sense the supernal philosophic destiny of their Fraternity.

The modern Masonic order can be traced back to a period in European history famous for its intrigue both political and sociological. Between the years 1600 and 1800, mysterious agents moved across the face of the Continent. The forerunner of modern thought was beginning to make its appearance and all Europe was passing through the throes of internal dissension and reconstruction. Democracy was in its infancy, yet its potential power was already being felt. Thrones were beginning to totter. The aristocracy of Europe was like the old man on Sinbad's back: it was becoming more unbearable with every passing day. Although upon the surface national governments were seemingly able to cope with the situation, there was a definite undercurrent of impending change; and out of the masses, long patient under the yoke of oppression, were rising up the champions of religious, philosophic, and political liberty. These led the factions of the dissatisfied: people with legitimate grievances against the intolerance of the church and the oppression of the crown. Out of this struggle for expression materialized certain definite ideals, the same which have now come to be considered peculiarly Masonic.

The divine prerogatives of humanity were being crushed out by the three great powers of ignorance, superstition, and fear—ignorance, the power of the mob; fear, the power of the despot; and superstition, the power of the church. Between the thinker and personal liberty loomed the three "ruffians" or personifications of impediment-the torch, the crown, and the tiara. Brute force, kingly power, and ecclesiastical persuasion became the agents of a great oppression, the motive of a deep unrest, the deterrent to all progress. It was unlawful to think, well-nigh fatal to philosophize, rank heresy to doubt. To question the infallibility of the existing order was to invite the persecution of the church and the state. These together incited the populace, which thereupon played the role of executioner for these arch-enemies of human liberty. Thus the ideal of democracy assumed a definite form during these stormy periods of European history. This democracy was not only a vision but a retrospection, not only a looking forward but a gazing backward upon better days and the effort to project those better days into the unborn tomorrow. The ethical, political, and philosophical institutions of antiquity with their constructive effect upon the whole structure of the state were noble examples of possible conditions. It became the dream of the oppressed, consequently, to re-establish a golden age upon the earth, an age where the thinker could think in safety and the dreamer dream in peace; when the wise should lead and the simple follow, yet all dwell together in fraternity and industry.

During this period several books were in circulation which, to a certain degree, registered the pulse of the time. One of these documents—More's *Utopia*—was the picture of a new age when heavenly conditions should prevail upon the earth. This ideal of establishing good in the world savored of blasphemy, however, for in that day heaven alone it was assumed could be good. Men did not seek to establish heavenly conditions upon earth, but rather earthly conditions in heaven. According to popular concept, the more the individual suffered the torments of the damned upon earth, the more he would enjoy the blessedness of heaven. Life was a period of chastisement and earthly happiness an unattainable mirage. More's *Utopia* thus came as a definite blow to autocratic pretensions and attitudes, giving impulse to the material emphasis which was to follow in succeeding centuries.

Another prominent figure of this period was Sir Walter Raleigh, who paid with his life for high treason against the crown. Raleigh was tried and, though the charge was never proved, was executed. Before Raleigh went to trial, it was known that he must die and that no defense could save him. His treason against the crown was of a character very different, however, from that which history records. Raleigh was a member of a secret society or body of men who were already moving irresistibly forward under the banner of democracy, and for that affiliation he died a felon's death. The actual reason for Raleigh's death sentence was his refusal to reveal the identity either of that great political organization of which he was a member or his *confreres* who were fighting the dogma of faith and the divine right of kings. On the title page of the first edition of Raleigh's *History of the World,* we accordingly find a mass of intricate emblems framed between two great columns. When the executioner sealed his lips forever, Raleigh's silence, while it added to the discomfiture of his persecutors, assured the safety of his colleagues.

One of the truly great minds of that secret fraternity—in

fact, the moving spirit of the whole enterprise-was Sir Francis Bacon, whose prophecy of the coming age forms the theme of his *New Atlantis* and whose vision of the reformation of knowledge finds expression in the *Novum Organum Scientiarum*, the new organ of science or thought. In the engraving at the beginning of the latter volume may be seen the little ship of progressivism sailing out between the Pillars of Galen and Avicenna, venturing forth beyond the imaginary pillars of church and state upon the unknown sea of human liberty. It is significant that Bacon was appointed by the British Crown to protect its interests in the new American Colonies beyond the sea. We find him writing of this new land, dreaming of the day when a new world and a new government of the philosophic elect should be established there, and scheming to consummate that end when the time should be ripe. Upon the title page of the 1640 edition of Bacon's *Advancement of Learning* is a Latin motto to the effect that he was the third great mind since Plato. Bacon was a member of the same group to which Sir Walter Raleigh belonged, but Bacon's position as Lord High Chancellor protected him from Raleigh's fate. Every effort was made, however, to humiliate and discredit him. At last, in the sixty-sixth year of his life, having completed the work which held him in England, Bacon feigned death and passed over into Germany, there to guide the destinies of his philosophic and political fraternity for nearly twenty-five years before his actual demise.

Other notable characters of the period are Montaigne, Ben Jonson, Marlowe, and the great Franz Joseph of Transylvania—the latter one of the most important as well as active figures in all this drama, a man who ceased fighting Austria to retire into a monastery in Transylvania from which to direct the activities of his secret society. One political upheaval followed another, the grand climax of this political unrest culminating in the French Revolution, which was directly precipitated by the attacks upon the person of Alessandro Cagliostro. The "divine" Cagliostro, by far the most picturesque character of the time, has the distinction of being more maligned than any other person of history. Tried by the Inquisition for founding a Masonic lodge in the city of Rome, Cagliostro was sentenced to die, a sentence later commuted by the Pope to life imprisonment in the old castle of San Leo. Shortly after his incarceration, Cagliostro disappeared and the story was circulated that he had been strangled in an attempt to escape from prison. In reality, however, he was liberated and returned to his Masters in the East. But Cagliostro—the idol of France, surnamed "the Father of the Poor," who never received anything from anyone and gave everything to everyone—was most adequately revenged. Though the people little understood this inexhaustible pitcher of bounty which poured forth benefits and never required replenishment, they remembered him in the day of their power.

Cagliostro founded the Egyptian Rite of Freemasonry, which received into its mysteries many of the French nobility and was regarded favorably by the most learned minds of Europe. Having established the Egyptian Rite, Cagliostro declared himself to be an agent of the order of the Knights Templars and to have received initiation from them on the Isle of Malta. (See *Morals and Dogma,* in which Albert Pike quotes

Eliphas Levi on Cagliostro's affiliation with the Templars.) Called upon the carpet by the Supreme Council of France, it was demanded of Cagliostro that he prove by what authority he had founded a Masonic lodge in Paris independent of the Grand Orient. Of such surpassing mentality was Cagliostro that the Supreme Council found it difficult to secure an advocate qualified to discuss with Cagliostro philosophic Masonry and the ancient Mysteries he claimed to represent. The Court de Gebelin—the greatest Egyptologist of his day and an authority on ancient philosophies-was chosen as the outstanding scholar. A time was set and the Brethren convened. Attired in an Oriental coat and a pair of violet-colored breeches, Cagliostro was haled before this council of his peers. The Court de Gebelin asked three questions and then sat down, admitting himself disqualified to interrogate a man so much his superior in every branch of learning. Cagliostro then took the floor, revealing to the assembled Masons not only his personal qualifications, but prophesying the future of France. He foretold the fall of the French throne, the Reign of Terror, and the fall of the Bastille. At a later time he revealed the dates of the death of Marie Antoinette and the King, and also the advent of Napoleon. Having finished his address, Cagliostro made a spectacular exit, leaving the French Masonic lodge in consternation and utterly incapable of coping with the profundity of his reasoning. Though no longer regarded as a ritual in Freemasonry, the Egyptian Rite is available and all who read it will recognize its author to have been no more a charlatan than was Plato.

Then appears that charming "first American

gentleman," Dr. Benjamin Franklin, who together with the Marquis de Lafayette, played an important role in this drama of empires. While in France, Dr. Franklin was privileged to receive definite esoteric instruction. It is noteworthy that Franklin was the first in America to reprint Anderson's *Constitutions of the Free-Masons,* which is a most prized work on the subject, though its accuracy is disputed. Through all this stormy period, these impressive figures come and go, part of a definite organization of political and religious thought—a functioning body of philosophers represented in Spain by no less an individual than Cervantes, in France by Cagliostro and St.-Germain, in Germany by Gichtel and Andreae, in England by Bacon, More, and Raleigh, and in America by Washington and Franklin. Coincident with the Baconian agitation in England, the *Fama Fraternitatis* and *Confessio Fraternitatis* appeared in Germany, both of these works being contributions to the establishment of a philosophic government upon the earth. One of the outstanding links between the Rosicrucian Mysteries of the Middle Ages and modern Masonry is Elias Ashmole, the historian of the Order of the Garter and the first Englishman to compile the alchemical writings of the English chemists.

The foregoing may seem to be a useless recital of inanities, but its purpose is to impress upon the reader's mind the philosophical and political situation in Europe at the time of the inception of the Masonic order. A philosophic clan, as it were, which had moved across the face of Europe under such names as the "Illuminati" and the "Rosicrucians," had undermined in a subtle manner the entire structure of regal and sacerdotal supremacy. The founders of Freemasonry were all men who were more or less identified with the progressive tendencies of their day. Mystics, philosophers, and alchemists were all bound together with a secret tie and dedicated to the emancipation of humanity from ignorance and oppression. In my researches among ancient books and manuscripts, I have pieced together a little story of probabilities which has a direct bearing upon the subject. Long before the establishment of Freemasonry as a fraternity, a group of mystics founded in Europe what was called the "Society of Unknown Philosophers." Prominent among the profound thinkers who formed the membership of this society were the alchemists, who were engaged in transmuting the political and religious "base metal" of Europe into ethical and spiritual "gold"; the Qabbalists who, as investigators of the superior orders of Nature, sought to discover a stable foundation for human government; and lastly the astrologers who, from a study of the procession of the heavenly bodies, hoped to find therein the rational archetype for all mundane procedure. Here and there is to be found a character who contacted this society. By some it is believed that both Martin Luther and also that great mystic, Philip Melanchthon, were connected with it. The first edition of the King James Bible, which was edited by Francis Bacon and prepared under Masonic supervision, bears more Mason's marks than the Cathedral of Strasburg. The same is true respecting the Masonic symbolism found in the first English edition of Josephus' *History of the Jews*.

For some time, the Society of Unknown Philosophers moved extraneous to the church. Among the fathers of the church, however, were a great number of scholarly and intelligent men who were keenly interested in philosophy and ethics, prominent among them being the Jesuit Father, Athanasius Kircher, who is recognized as one of the great scholars of his day. Both a Rosicrucian and also a member of the Society of Unknown Philosophers, as revealed by the cryptograms in his writings, Kircher was in harmony with this program of philosophic reconstruction. Since learning was largely limited to churchmen, this body of philosophers soon developed an overwhelming preponderance of ecclesiastics in its membership. The original anti-ecclesiastical ideals of the society were thus speedily reduced to an innocuous state and the organization gradually converted into an actual auxiliary of the church. A small portion of the membership, however, ever maintained an aloofness from the literati of the faith, for it represented an unorthodox class—the alchemists, Rosicrucians, Qabbalists, and magicians. This latter group accordingly retired from the outer body of the society that had thus come to be known as the "Order of the Golden and Rose Cross" and whose adepts were elevated to the dignity of Knights of the Golden Stone. Upon the withdrawal of these initiated adepts, a powerful clerical body remained which possessed considerable of the ancient lore but in many instances lacked the "keys" by which this symbolism could be interpreted. As this body continued to increase in temporal power, its philosophical power grew correspondingly less.

The smaller group of adepts that had withdrawn from the order remained inactive apparently, having retired to what they termed the "House of the Holy Spirit," where they were enveloped by certain "mists" impenetrable to the eyes of the profane. Among these reclusive adepts must be included such well-known Rosicrucians as Robert Fludd, Eugenius Philalethes, John Heydon, Michael Maier, and Henri Khunrath. These adepts in their retirement constituted a loosely organized society which, though lacking the solidarity of a definite fraternity, occasionally initiated a candidate and met annually at a specified place. It was the Comte de Chazal, an initiate of this order, who "raised" Dr. Sigismund Bacstrom while the latter was on the Isle of Mauritius. In due time, the original members of the order passed on, after first entrusting their secrets to carefully chosen successors. In the meantime, a group of men in England, under the leadership of such mystics as Ashmole and Fludd, had resolved upon repopularizing the ancient learning and reclassifying philosophy in accordance with Bacon's plan for a world encyclopedia. These men had undertaken to reconstruct ancient Platonic and Gnostic mysticism, but were unable to attain their objective for lack of information. Elias Ashmole may have been a member of the European order of Rosicrucians and as such evidently knew that in various parts of Europe there were isolated individuals who were in possession of the secret doctrine handed down in unbroken line from the ancient Greeks and Egyptians through Boetius, the early Christian Church, and the Arabians.

The efforts of the English group to contact such individuals were evidently successful. Several initiated Rosicrucians were brought from the mainland to England, where they remained for a considerable time designing the symbolism of Freemasonry and incorporating into the rituals of the order the same divine principles and philosophy that had formed the inner doctrine of all great secret societies from the time of the Eleusinia in Greece. In fact, the Eleusinian Mysteries themselves continued in Christendom until the sixth century after Christ, after which they passed into the custody of the Arabians, as attested by the presence of Masonic symbols and figures upon early Mohammedan monuments. The adepts brought over from the Continent to sit in council with the English philosophers were initiates of the Arabian rites and thus through them the Mysteries were ultimately returned to Christendom. Upon completion of the by-laws of the new fraternity, the initiates retired again into Central Europe, leaving a group of disciples to develop the outer organization, which was to function as a sort of screen to conceal the activities of the esoteric order.

Such, in brief, is the story to be pieced together from the fragmentary bits of evidence available. The whole structure of Freemasonry is founded upon the activities of this secret society of Central European adepts; whom the studious Mason will find to be the definite "link" between the modern Craft and the Ancient Wisdom. The outer body of Masonic philosophy was merely the veil of this qabbalistic order whose members were the custodians of the true Arcanum. Does this inner and secret brotherhood of initiates still exist independent of the Freemasonic order? Evidence points to the fact that it does, for these august adepts are the actual preservers of those secret operative processes of the Greeks whereby the illumination and completion of the individual is effected. They are the veritable guardians of the "Lost Word"—the Keepers of the inner Mystery-and the Mason who searches for and discovers them is rewarded beyond all mortal estimation.

In the preface to a book entitled *Long-Livers*, published in 1772, Eugenius Philalethes, the Rosicrucian initiate, thus addresses his Brethren of the Most Ancient and Most Honorable Fraternity of the Free Masons: "Remember that you are the Salt of the Earth, the Light of the World, and the Fire of the Universe. You are living Stones, built up a Spiritual House, who believe and rely on the chief Lapis Angularis which the refractory and disobedient Builders disallowed. You are called from Darkness to Light; you are a chosen Generation, a royal Priesthood. This makes you, my dear Brethren, fit Companions for the greatest Kings; and no wonder, since the King of Kings hath condescended to make you so to himself, compared to whom the mightiest and most haughty Princes of the Earth are but as Worms, and that not so much as we are all Sons of the same One Eternal Father, by whom all Things were made; but inasmuch as we do the Will of his and our Father which is in Heaven. You see now your high Dignity; you see what you are; act accordingly, and show yourselves (*what you are*) MEN, and walk worthy the high Profession to which you are called.   * * * Remember, then, what the great End we all aim at is: Is it not to be happy *here* and *hereafter?* For they both depend on each other. The Seeds of that eternal Peace and Tranquility and everlasting Repose must be sown in this Life; and he that would glorify and enjoy the Sovereign Good then must learn to do it now, and from contemplating the Creature gradually ascend to adore the Creator."

Of all obstacles to surmount in matters of rationality, the

most difficult is that of prejudice. Even the casual observer must realize that the true wealth of Freemasonry lies in its mysticism. The average Masonic scholar, however, is fundamentally opposed to a mystical interpretation of his symbols, for he shares the attitude of the modern mind in its general antipathy towards transcendentalism. A most significant fact, however, is that those Masons who have won signal honors for their contributions to the Craft have been transcendentalists almost without exception. It is quite incredible, moreover, that any initiated Brother, when presented with a copy of *Morals and Dogma* upon the conferment of his fourteenth degree, can read that volume and yet maintain that his order is not identical with the Mystery Schools of the first ages. Much of the writings of Albert Pike are extracted from the books of the French magician, Eliphas Levi, one of the greatest transcendentalists of modern times. Levi was an occultist, a metaphysician, a Platonic philosopher, who by the rituals of magic invoked even the spirit of Apollonius of Tyana, and yet Pike has inserted in his *Morals and Dogma* whole pages, and even chapters, practically verbatim. To Pike the following remarkable tribute was paid by Stirling Kerr, Jr., 33* Deputy for the Inspector-General for the District of Columbia, upon crowning with laurel the bust of Pike in the House of the Temple: "Pike was an oracle greater than that of Delphi. He was Truth's minister and priest. His victories were those of peace. Long may his memory live in the hearts of the Brethren." Affectionately termed "Albertus Magnus" by his admirers, Pike wrote of Hermeticism and alchemy and hinted at the Mysteries of the Temple. Through his zeal and unflagging energy, American Freemasonry was raised from comparative obscurity to become the most powerful organization in the land. Though Pike, a transcendental thinker, was the recipient of every honor that the Freemasonic bodies of the world could confer, the modern Mason is loath to admit that transcendentalism has any place in Freemasonry. This is an attitude filled with embarrassment and inconsistency, for whichever way the Mason turns he is confronted by these inescapable issues of philosophy and the Mysteries. Yet withal he dismisses the entire subject as being more or less a survival of primitive superstitions.

The Mason who would discover the *Lost Word* must remember, however, that in the first ages—every neophyte was a man of profound learning and unimpeachable character, who for the sake of wisdom and virtue had faced death unafraid and had triumphed over those limitations of the flesh which bind most mortals to the sphere of mediocrity. In those days the rituals were not put on by degree teams who handled candidates as though they were perishable commodities, but by priests deeply versed in the lore of their cults. Not one Freemason out of a thousand could have survived the initiations of the pagan rites, for the tests were given in those strenuous days when men were men and death the reward of failure. The neophyte of the Druid Mysteries was set adrift in a small boat to battle with the stormy sea, and unless his knowledge of natural law enabled him to quell the storm as did Jesus upon the Sea of Galilee, he returned no more. In the Egyptian rites of Serapis, it was required of the neophyte that he cross an unbridged chasm in the temple floor. In other words, if unable by magic to sustain himself in the air without visible support, he fell headlong into a volcanic crevice, there to die of heat and suffocation. In one part of the Mithraic rites, the candidate seeking admission to the inner sanctuary was required to pass through a closed door by dematerialization. The philosopher who has authenticated the reality of ordeals such as these no longer entertains the popular error that the performance of "miracles" is confined solely to Biblical characters. "Do you still ask," writes Pike, "if it has its secrets and mysteries? It is certain that something in the Ancient Initiations was regarded as of immense value, by such Intellects as Herodotus, Plutarch and Cicero. The Magicians of Egypt were able to imitate several of the miracles wrought by Moses; and the Science of the Hierophants of the mysteries produced effects that to the Initiated seemed Mysterious and supernatural." (See *Legenda for the Twenty-eighth Degree.*)

It becomes self-evident that he who passed successfully through these arduous tests involving both natural and also supernatural hazards was a man apart in his community. Such an initiate was deemed to be more than human, for he had achieved where countless ordinary mortals, having failed, had returned no more. Let us hear the words of Apuleius when admitted into the Temple of Isis, as recorded in *The Metamorphosis, or Golden Ass:* "Then also the priest, all the profane being removed, taking hold of me by the hand, brought me to the penetralia of the temple, clothed in a new linen garment. Perhaps, inquisitive reader, you will very anxiously ask me what was then said and done? I would tell you, if it could be lawfully told; you should know it, if it was lawful for you to hear it. But both ears and the tongue are guilty of rash curiosity.

Nevertheless, I will not keep you in suspense with religious desire, nor torment you with long-continued anxiety. Hear, therefore, but believe what is true. *I approached to the confines of death, and having trod on the threshold of Proserpine, I returned from it, being carried through all the elements. At midnight I saw the sun shining with a splendid light; and I manifestly drew near to the Gods beneath, and the Gods above, and proximately adored them.* Behold, I have narrated to you things, of which, though heard, it is nevertheless necessary that you should be ignorant. I will, therefore, only relate that which may be enunciated to the understanding of the profane without a crime."

Kings and princes paid homage to the initiate—the "newborn" man, the favorite of the gods. The initiate had actually entered into the presence of the divine beings. He had "died" and been "raised" again into the radiant sphere of everlasting light. Seekers after wisdom journeyed across great continents to hear his words and his sayings were treasured with the revelations of oracles. It was even esteemed an honor to receive from such a one an inclination of the head, a kindly smile or a gesture of approbation. Disciples gladly paid with their lives for the Master's word of praise and died of a broken heart at his rebuke. On one occasion, Pythagoras became momentarily irritated because of the seeming stupidity of one of his students. The Master's displeasure so preyed upon the mind of the humiliated youth that, drawing a knife from the folds of his garment, he committed suicide. So greatly moved was Pythagoras by the incident that never from that time on was he known to lose patience with any of his followers regardless of the provocation.

With a smile of paternal indulgence the venerable Master, who senses the true dignity of the mystic tie, should gravely incline the minds of the Brethren towards the sublimer issues of the Craft. The officer who would serve his lodge most effectively must realize that he is of an order apart from other men, that he is the keeper of an awful secret, that the chair upon which he sits is the seat of immortals, and that if he would be a worthy successor to those Master Masons of other ages, his thoughts must be measured by the profundity of Pythagoras and the lucidity of Plato. Enthroned in the radiant East, the Worshipful Master is the "Light" of his lodge—the representative of the gods, one of that long line of hierophants who, through the blending of their rational powers with the reason of the Ineffable, have been accepted into the Great School. This high priest after an ancient order must realize that those before him are not merely a gathering of properly tested men, but the custodians of an eternal lore, the guardians of a sacred truth, the perpetuators of an ageless wisdom, the consecrated servants of a living God, the wardens of a Supreme Mystery.

A new day is dawning for Freemasonry. From the insufficiency of theology and the hopelessness of materialism, men are turning to seek the God of philosophy. In this new era wherein the old order of things is breaking down and the individual is rising triumphant above the monotony of the masses, there is much work to be accomplished. The "Temple Builder" is needed as never before. A great reconstruction period is at hand; the debris of a fallen culture must be cleared away; the old footings must be found again that a new Temple significant of a new revelation of Law may be raised thereon. This is the peculiar work of the Builder; this is the high duty for which he was called out of the world; this is the noble enterprise for which he was "raised" and given the tools of his Craft. By thus doing his part in the reorganization of society, the workman may earn his "wages" as all good Masons should. A new light is breaking in the East, a more glorious day is at hand. The rule of the philosophic elect-the dream of the ages-will yet be realized and is not far distant. To her loyal sons, Freemasonry sends this clarion call: "Arise ye, the day of labor is at band; the Great Work awaits completion, and the days of man's life are few." Like the singing guildsman of bygone days, the Craft of the Builders marches victoriously down the broad avenues of Time. Their song is of labor and glorious endeavor; their anthem is of toil and industry; they rejoice in their noble destiny, for they are the Builders of cities, the Hewers of worlds, the Master Craftsmen of the universe!

ROSICRUCIANISM IS FREEMASONRY

By Harold Voorhis

There seems to be a decided interest in Rosicrucianism springing up among Masonic students. The mystery of the Rosy Cross, as it is more generally known, is apparently becoming more mysterious. The terms Rosicrucian and Brother of the Rosy Cross are in reality synonymous, but the first term often intimates a reference to the "Order" itself, while the second connotes a relationship to the Rose Croix, now the Eighteenth Degree of the Scottish Rite of Masonry. This revival of interest manifests itself every few years with added zest and is caused, usually, by a new investigator appearing upon the horizon with new (*or at least more*) facts; combined also with the ascertain activity within the modern Rosicrucian societies.

Lately I have perused several important writings containing opinions on the existing complex and conflicting data related to this obscure subject. These show, to my own satisfaction at least, that the history of Rosicrucianism and Freemasonry has a common spiritual descent, a common mystery and at one time, during the early years of the two movements, had a common motive.

The mere mention of the word "Rosicrucian" in occult circles immediately produces an atmosphere of awe. Individuals who are the most sound logicians in every other branch of research, almost without exception begin to float on air, and, for the most part, enjoy it, as soon as this subject is broached. As Arthur Edward Waite has said:

> *Perhaps there has never been a realm of inquiry which has been colonized to such an extent by fools and knaves of speculation. If there has been one other, it is that which adjoins with no intervening boundary - I mean Emblematic Freemasonry.*

The reason for this condition is not difficult to see. It is a condition of mind, resulting from the perusal of the many works on the subject by the great students who have written so deeply and voluminously on not only the subject of Rosicrucianism itself, but also on the outstanding men and, in a few instances, the women involved in the manifold workings of "The Order of the Rosy Cross."

It would almost seem that every person of note as an occult scholar from the year 1500 to 1800 (*and possibly further*) has been in some manner connected with the "Order." Independent schools of or allied to Rosicrucianism have developed an individual literature portion to each school - thus complicating the development of a system rather than clarifying it. Says Waite:

> *The great spiritual symbolism which has come down to us through several houses of tradition, is not, I think, communicated in a plenary sense by any one school; it is rather the harmony of all.*

A sentence once written in the thirteenth century by that

unsurpassed thinker, Roger Bacon, can be applied very pertinently to Rosicrucianism. He said:

> *The subjects in question are weighty and unusual, they stand in need of the grace and favor accorded to human frailty . . . for I am speaking of the sophistical authorities of the irrational multitude, men who are authorities in an equivocal sense, even as the eye carved in stone or painted on canvas has the name but not the quality of an eye.*

The eminent English Mystic, Waite already quoted, says further:

> *The touchstone is always life, and for this reason antiquity per se is not a test of value. There would be no Hidden Mystery of the Rosy Cross if it had not suffered successive transmutations, adjusting a change of venture to a new heart of motive. I think, indeed, that it has died many times and has been as often reborn, even a little "nearer to the heart's desire."*

Anderson, whose *Book of Constitutions* was first published in 1723, gives a source for Masonic origins of which many subsequent writers have availed themselves down to the present day. The representations made by these good brethren of earlier days do not bear critical analysis in some respects, in spite of the fact that we do not question their motives nor the sincerity of their beliefs. One statement concerning the origin of Freemasonry has to do with its beginnings in the Garden of Eden, for Anderson says:

> *Adam, our first Parent, created after the Image of God, the*

41

Great Architect of the Universe, must have had the Liberal Sciences, particularly Geometry, written on his Heart; for even since the Fall, we find the Principles of it in the Hearts of his Offspring, and which, in process of time, have drawn forth into a convenient Method of Propositions, by observing the Laws of Proportion taken from Mechanism: So that as the Mechanical Arts gave occasion to the Learned to reduce the Elements of Geometry into Method, this noble Science thus reduc'd, is the Foundation of all those Arts (particularly of Masonry and Architecture), *and the rule by which they are conducted and perform'd, etc., etc., etc.*

In the dedication of *The Constitution*, J. T. Desaguliers, Deputy Grand Master, takes pains to say that he needed not to tell his Grace of Montagu, to whom it was addressed,

> *. . . what Pains our learned AUTHOR has taken in compiling and digesting this Book from the old RECORDS, and how accurately he has compar'd and made everything agreeable to History and Chronology, so as to render these NEW CONSTITUTIONS a just and exact Account of MASONRY from the Beginning of the World to Your Grace's MASTERSHIP.*

The views of Anderson, and those of later writers who followed him blindly, or elaborated upon the beauteous concepts of their times, are no longer accepted. In fact we are hard put to prove our existence prior to the Norman Conquest, and it is not until we reach the year 1390 A. D. that we first find documentary evidence - *The Regius Poem*, also known as the

Halliwell MS., now preserved in the British Museum. A few of these early Old Charges are the only definite evidence we have.

Rosicrucianism, however, has numerous documents relating to its activities, and especially during the two centuries prior to the year 1717, when speculative Freemasonry established this date as the foundation stone of a new dispensation. If we accepted the evidence offered by Spencer Lewis, the Rosicrucian Order can be traced back to King Thothmes III, B.C. 1500. However, let us put aside this speculation as to very ancient origins and content ourselves with the later history.

It cannot be refuted that, in the century prior to the formation of the premier Grand Lodge of England, many eminent men were practicing Rosicrucianism, not only in England but also in Germany, France, Holland and possibly other countries.

The word "Rosicrucian" first appears in print in 1614, and shortly thereafter the so-called Order first took form as a permanent organization through a man known as Christian Rosenkreutz whose date of birth appears to have been about 1378, although his *Fama* and *Confessio* did not attract attention until two hundred and fifty years later upon its original publication.[1]

---

[1] The Fama Fraternitatis, which is believed to have been written in the year 1610, but which apparently did not appear in print until 1614, although an earlier edition is suspected by some authorities. Manly P. Hall, An Encyclopedic Outline of Masonic, Hermetic, Qabbalistic, Rosicrucian and Symbolic Philosophy, 1928.

There is no exact period of commencement of the Rosicrucians as an Order, as there is in Freemasonry. Every well-informed Mason recognizes the date 1717. There can be no misunderstanding that, as that time the first Grand Lodge of Masons appeared. The best we can say about Rosicrucianism is that Rosy Cross literature appeared in German and Latin between 1614 and 1616 - affirming that a secret and mysterious Order had existed in Germany for some two centuries. These writings marked the entrance of Rosicrucianism into the daylight of contemporaneous criticism and attack.

To acquaint those interested with this branch of learning, Thomas De Quincey, in 1824, wrote a work entitled *Historico-Critical Inquiry into the Origin of the Rosicrucians and the Freemasons*. While this served as an excellent introduction to the subject, it was, to quote Waite,

> *A mere transcript from an exploded German savant, whose facts are tortured in the interest of a somewhat arbitrary hypothesis.*

The first serious treatment of the subject in English, from an historical standpoint, was Hargrave Jennings' *The Rosicrucians, Their Rites and Mysteries*, 1870. It had gone into many editions and is still a so-called textbook on Rosicrucianism. The two-volume edition of 1887 is considered the most desirable.

This treatment has been superseded by *The Real History of the Rosicrucians*, 1887, by Arthur Edward Waite and by another work written many years afterward on this subject from the pen of the same author (*really his magnum opus*), *The Brotherhood of the Rosy Cross*, 1924. This book is a most exhaustive treatise, especially in the treatment of the material whereof this so-called "Order" is built.

There is at least one excellent work in another language by Fr. Wittemans, D.L., covering the history of the Rosicrucians - but, so far, it is not available in English.

In America a writer, whose work on this subject in connection with Freemasonry has been taken seriously, is Brother Ossian Lang, Grand Historian, of the Grand Lodge of New York State. A small pamphlet reprinted from the proceedings of the Grand Lodge of New York, 1918, written by Brother Lang, gives data purporting proof of a Rosicrucian derivation of Freemasonry.

In the recent work of Manly P. Hall, the subject of Rosicrucianism is taken up by the author in the chapter headed *"The Fraternity of the Rosy Cross,"* by formulation of four postulates. The material has been carefully selected from a very wide range of works and excellently arranged.

Rosicrucianism first appeared in Germany (*in the City of Cassel*) in the latter part of the sixteenth century and came into public light, as already mentioned, in 1614. After arousing a great deal of interest in that country for about ten years, the mysteries of the Rosy Cross died down, and, because of the departure of several of the Rosicrucian adepts to India,[2] the struggle for "thought freedom" was shifted to the Netherlands,

---

[2] See the notes on the Latin pamphlet by Henrieus Neuhusius, 1618, in Waite's Occult Sciences, 1891, p. 210.

where it had been going on slowly for a quarter of a century. Persons of the highest classes of society met in palatial structures under the Rosicrucian banner at both Amsterdam and The Hague in 1622. Some of these persons ran afoul of the law of the land and were haled into court on various charges.

About this time, according to Wittemans, Frederic Henry, Stadtholder, who leaned toward the occult, and who no doubt saw a "writing on the wall," shifted his protection from Rosicrucianism to Freemasonry.[3]

In France there was no Rosicrucian activity until about 1623, when, after a first public announcement, the Rosicrucians became embroiled in arguments with the Jesuit Fathers. Descartes and Abbe de Villars were about the only two flaming spots of French Rosicrucianism of this period and, as they have not the slightest connection with Freemasonry, we turn our attention to England.

Concerning Rosicrucianism in England, Wittemans remarks that:

> *The efforts of the Rosicrucians to erect a new spiritual temple of humanity, which failed in Germany, the Netherlands and France, were destined to be crowned with success in England. In the latter country the free development of human thought was not hampered by orthodoxy and, there, resulted in a spiritual movement that afterward found expression in Freemasonry, the universal*

---

[3] Certain data in the work cited concern an ancient Masonic lodge in Amsterdam of great antiquity, have a bearing on this subject, and may bring out some interesting light on Freemasonry in the Netherlands.

temple of wisdom and fraternity.

Some time between 1614 and 1620, according to Waite, Robert Fludd, an English philosopher, physician, chemist, mechanic, anatomist, mathematician and astrologer, having been influenced by Maier became a "convert" to Rosicrucian thought.

He at once began writing on the subject and there appeared in 1616 his *Apologia,* a defense of Rosicrucianism. This was followed by a dozen or more other works on Rosicrucianism over a period of some twenty years. There are some (*Dr. W. Wynn Westcott, for instance*) who believe that Fludd was the first English Magus of the Brotherhood. At any rate, Fludd, together with Lord Verulam, better known as Francis Bacon, formed an English Rosicrucian Society in which Bacon, though secretly, played the principal role.

Bacon was 57 years old when Elias Ashmole, the famous English astrologer, was born and of whom we have positive proof of his being "made a Freemason" at Warrington in 1646. Bacon, however, died in 1626 at the age of 65 years, without, so far as we have any positive evidence, ever having been "made a Freemason."

Bacon is believed by many to have been the real author of the works attributed to Shakespeare and to have superintended the English translation of the Bible. He was the author of many works of a philosophical nature. His only connection with our story, however, is in relation to certain theories advanced by various writers that Freemasonry was either partially or totally shaped by him. To such Waite says:

> *The attempt to explain Freemasonry - Emblematical, Speculative and Figurative - as a new birth in time of the Order of the Rosy Cross has passed into desuetude, and yet there is evident - for it manifests now and again sporadically - a certain unsatisfied feeling, as if the last word still remained to be said. So also is there a feeling that in some way, occult and unproven, a shaping influence was exercised by Francis Bacon, Lord Verulam, on the first beginnings of the Masonic Order. I do not suppose the last word has been said on this subject either, but it is clear to my mind that it must be one of negation This thesis was started by Nicolai, in an appendix on the origin of Freemasonry attached to an Essay on the Knights Templar. The foundation is Bacon's unfinished romance* The New Atlantis, *written late in life and published posthumously.*

This view is not taken by either Fr. Wittemans or the Rev. F. de P. Castells of England. Bro. Castells, who is engaged at present on works concerning the origin of the Masonic degrees, supports, with modifications and amplifications, the views of Mrs. Henry Pott as advanced in her *Francis Bacon and His Secret Society.* Fr. Wittemans says:

> *He [Bacon] ranks first among those who made Freemasonry heir to the Rosicrucian philosophy, at the time when the Masonic body underwent a reformation in the XVIIth century.*

Manly P. Hall contributes this information:

> *Johann Valentin Andreae is generally reputed to be the*

author of the Confessio. *It is a much-mooted question, however, whether Andreae did not permit his name to be used as a pseudonym by Sir Francis Bacon. Apropos of this subject are two extremely significant references occurring in the introduction to that remarkable potpourri* The Anatomy of Melancholy. *This volume first appeared in 1621 from the pen of Democritus Junior, who was afterward identified as Robert Burton who, in turn, was a suspected intimate of Sir Francis Bacon. One reference archly suggests that at the time of publishing* The Anatomy of Melancholy *in 1621 the founder of the Fraternity of R. C. was still alive. This statement - concealed from general recognition by its textual involvement - has escaped the notice of most students of Rosicrucianism. In the same work there also appears a short footnote of stupendous import. It contains merely the words: "Joh. Valent. Andreas, Lord Verulam." This single line definitely relates Johann Valentin Andreae to Sir Francis Bacon, who was Lord Verulam, and by its punctuation intimates that they are one and the same individual.*

As Robert Macoy, the well-known Masonic writer, believed that Andreae was the true founder of Rosicrucianism, so, following the reasoning of Mr. Hall, indications appear that Bacon was responsible for even more than is generally suspected in the launching of our project. Further references along similar lines are found in Godfrey Higgins' *Anacalypsis*, and in the writings of the late Frank C. Higgins.

No matter which view one considers correct, it is most certainly a fact that Bacon lived at a time in which the minds of the forefathers of organized Masonry had their setting - a time in which it appears that English Rosicrucianism waned and Freemasonry assumed its outward role and continued on - and, according to Bro. Castells, soon worked out its role.

To go into this matter further would entail a complete review of Waite's, Castells', Mrs. Pott's and Fr. Wittemans' works, to say nothing of those quoted in this article. One must refer the reader to the writings of these individuals if interested in obtaining the latest views thereon. Wittemans' book, as indicated, is, unfortunately, not yet available in English.

The Rosicrucian connection with Freemasonry was considered in Quatuor Coronati Lodge, No. 2076, of London, in a paper written by Dr. Wynn Westcott in 1894.[4]

Edward Conder, Jr., Waite, Van der Gon, Alting, Raemaekers, Mrs. Pott and Castells all agree that Bacon and Rosicrucianism certainly had something to do with Freemasonry just prior to its "revival" of 1717. But so many opinions have been expressed on various phases of the subject that to cite any here would be burdensome reading.

Fr. Wittemans estimates that over twenty thousand books and articles have been written on Bacon's alleged authorship of Shakespeare's plays. It would be natural to suppose that there would also be an extensive literature on the Baconian theory of Masonic origin. Just the reverse however, is true. Although there is a distinct school of the Bacon-

---

[4] "The Rosicrucians, Their History and Aims, with reference to the alleged connection between Rosicrucians and Freemasonry," A. Q. C. vol. vii, p. 37.

Masonic origin theorists, it is supported by but few writers, and their contentions have received but meager support.

Many writers endeavor to prove that the Rosicrucians used many symbols traceable to ancient Masonry. This department of our subject is even more confusing, especially to minds not trained in symbology, but it cannot be denied by anyone familiar with the "teachings" of both "fraternities" that many similarities do exist. Basing their judgment on things symbolic, De Quincey and Buhle believed that Freemasonry was Rosicrucianism modified by those who introduced it from Germany into England.

Because of changes in ritual after the formation of the premier Grand Lodge, before which time Freemasonry and Rosicrucianism were supposedly closely allied, and the organization of the present or modern Rosicrucian societies, which appear to lack descent from the original "Order," those differences have broadened.

The recent work of Bro. Castells[5] has again brought these questions to the fore among Masonic students. Coupled with the fact that the Rose Croix Degree has been drawn into the discussion, we have the outpourings of the English and American societies working under the banner and the name of Rosicrucianism, so that the present period promises some interesting research into these absorbing topics.

---

[5] The works by the Rev. F. de P Castells referred to are his Antiquity on the Holy Royal Arch, 1927; the Origin of the Masonic Degrees, 1928; and The Historical Analysis of the Holy Royal Arch Ritual, 1929.

Freemasonry is defined as "*a beautiful system of morality, veiled in allegory and illustrated with symbols . . . Truth is its center. It is founded on the purest principles of Morality, Brotherly Love and Charity,*" which Rosicrucians "*have aimed to produce, in the crucible of spiritual alchemy, the perfect Man, who loves God above all, on whose heart the Christ has awakened and who has become a pillar of love and wisdom among his fellowmen,*" says Wittemans.

Where one "system" leaves off and the other begins cannot be precisely defined - like a mixture of water and glycerin, no one can tell by vision which is more in quantity. Rosicrucianism and Freemasonry, it seems, were once entwined. Since that time each has perceptibly changed in both spirit and matter. If they were definitely separated once, much more must be known to determine their points of separation. Even now their forms are not easily separated. The teaching of each "system" is not a clear and defined thing. Students of either school fail to present a positive agreement in aims or objects - and even less, the students of both.

The writer has not set down the above in a disparaging sense, but just the reverse. He has read many works on both subjects and feels that studies of this nature are far more important than the grinding out of meaningless "joining Masons." In fact, he feels that works such as Fr. Wittemans, are permanently valuable and hopes that his publication will be translated into the English language in the near future, so that it may take its proper place beside the work of Waite, Castells, Hall and others cited above. It is by far the most thorough and comprehensive work of its kind that has come to my attention and makes an excellent companion volume to Waite's *The Brotherhood of the Rosy Cross*. Its value, particularly to Masonic students, as well as to students of the Rosy Cross, lies in the great clarification it makes of the subject it covers.

Milton Keynes UK
Ingram Content Group UK Ltd.
UKHW011318300424
441995UK00021B/148